Drawing on a "cartography of allusions" from Egyptian, Native American, Vodou, jazz, and Anansian sources, and in creating a resonant journey that moves from Africa to the New World, from ancient worlds to our multifaceted contemporary world, T. J. Anderson III explores what it means to be "a stalker of history" and writes with authenticity, mythic imagination, and verve. With a culminating initiation ceremony that lets a story come and lets it go, Anderson writes in compelling rhythms and delineates how "writing" is "but a struggle to employ / the limits of speech." *Devonte Travels the Sorry Route* is a singular accomplishment that extends the range and enriches the depth of contemporary American poetry.

Arthur Sze, judge of the Omnidawn Open

Devonte Travels the Sorry Route works at the "limits of speech," syncopating the page to create not so much a textual work as an experience—of language. Language harnessed by history and histories, by myth, mathematics and alchemy, by pain and loss and, above all, by a formal control that allows these ideas to compete yet work together. The downward trajectory, the "sorry route," of Devonte, the anti- or un-hero, follows a path that appears, in these times, tragically inevitable for the many like him; a path which drives the narrative and provides the structure around which Anderson scores his poetry so as to countervail that overwhelming tragic trope. Here, in the interstices of time, in the shadow of failed empires past and present, we confront a poetry that wails and mourns like an angry jazz saxophone, weeps in the quiet blue hours, hips and hops across oceans, blasts through all that is impenetrable to shuffle off the yoke of history, crisscrossing and braiding the hidden beauty of lives that insist and resist. From jazz explosion to flattened blues notes, from the quiet refrain of ancestral laments to lyric couplets, *Devonte* leads the reader through time, as Ariadne, Anansi, Damballa and Toussaint jostle each other. At the journey's end we are charged and changed and, despite Devonte's "sorry route," strangely made more humble, more willing to resist and yet more compassionate. The un-heroism of Devonte becomes so much more admirable.

M. NourbeSe Philip

Devonte Takes the Sorry Route is T. J. Anderson III's newest collection and one of his finest. This book-length conversation and masquerade in four sections, via the voice and vision of his alter ego Devonte, melds the contemporary and historical, fusing high lyricism and the vernacular to draw forth the ritual and spiritual from everyday language and life, charging every moment it explores with resonant depth and power. Drafting "alchemic equations" Anderson creates a series of vessels through which to re-see the world illuminated by his poetry's singular "vessels."

John Keene

Devonte Travels the Sorry Route

Also by T. J. Anderson III

Cairo Workbook, Established Author Series, Willow Books, 2014.

River to Cross, The Backwaters Press, 2009.

Notes to Make the Sound Come Right: Four Innovators of Jazz Poetry,
University of Arkansas Press, 2004.

At Last Round Up, Chapbook Series, lift books, 1996.

Devonte Travels the Sorry Route

T.J. Anderson III

OMNIDAWN PUBLISHING
OAKLAND, CALIFORNIA
2019

Cover art: "Sorry Route," oil on canvas, Brian Counihan
Used by permission of artist
Contact: Brian Counihan <brian@communityhigh.net>

Cover and interior set in ITC Avant Garde Gothic Std and Perpetua Std

Cover and interior design by Gillian Olivia Blythe Hamel

Offset printed in the United States
by Sheridan Books, Chelsea, Michigan
On 55# Glatfelter B19 Antique
Acid Free Archival Quality Recycled Paper

Library of Congress Cataloging-in-Publication Data

Names: Anderson, T. J., 1958- author.
Title: Devonte travels the sorry route / T. J. Anderson III.
Description: Oakland, California : Omnidawn Publishing, [2019]
Identifiers: LCCN 2018040201 | ISBN 9781632430670 (pbk. : alk. paper)
Classification: LCC PS3551.N39477 A6 2019 | DDC 811/.6--dc23
LC record available at https://lccn.loc.gov/2018040201

Published by Omnidawn Publishing, Oakland, California
www.omnidawn.com   (510) 237-5472   (800) 792-4957
10 9 8 7 6 5 4 3 2 1
ISBN: 978-1-63243-067-0

Previous versions of these poems were published in Let the Bucket Down, January 2016,
when this manuscript was titled Dickerson Travels The Sorry Route: "Dickerson Prowls the
Alley," "Dickerson Wears a Canvas," Dickerson in the Crow's Nest," "Dickerson Travels the
Sorry Route," "Dickerson Unravels the Sari Root."

All art is collaborative.

For the Ancestors.
For Brian Counihan.
For Joseph Torra.

Table   of   Contents

We are over-rehearsed, accidents don't happen, but are explained, coincidences mount to reinforce effect. We haven't a clue where to begin each day we stutter forward, repeating one part, eliding another, remnants of worlds we incompletely reside.

Erica   Hunt

Ma mémoire sont des est entourée de sang. Ma mémoire a sa ceinture de cadaures.

Aimé   Césaire

You don't write your way out of the chaos. What you do is nail something down that will allow you to get further downstream.

Ed   Roberson

The   Impossible   Suture

Sound (first)

  then Music   *cyclical a way of sonic measure*

                                        arises out of darkness

as does breath
in fact, is it
black & w/hole if we
but listen.

   Wind plies us in multiple ways gusting

                                   through our body's sap

   The rise & ebb tone of earth at 136.1 Hz
   Vibratory snap, our DNA curative

suspended animation of beings pulsating
light to our cosmic home among the stars

Ariadne's golden belt a fabric astronautical
phosphorescent flight.

Kokopelli tricks it out
with bent horn,
phallic antler,
and cosmic straw

                                        Perhaps the last one...

But it's Nut in her lab coat draped that alchemizes
us shimmering cocoon as filament
                        khol lined night.

                                Maá Afra   Maá Afra

                It is Ptah, maker of things

we lose track of

                Anansi's web neural vines the story's translucent strands
        makes the Jacob's ladder ropes.

                                Maá Afra   Maá Afra
                                Maá Afra   Maá Afra
                                Maá Afra   Maá Afra
                                Maá Afra   Maá Afra
                                Maá Afra   Maá Afra
                                Maá Afra   Maá Afra

Curl of the ocean
Sentinel of wave cupping
the great arrival

The darkness of this music that punches through

canals of bodies,
                                                black
                                                black
avenues of bodies,   black
footways of
bodies
rivers of plasma,
lakes of thirst
                Turbulence   unceasing

oceans...oceans...oceans...oceans....oceans....oceans....

*

We witnessed a murky fog approaching
the ship's aft. I told the first mate to go about
but the current tugged us forward.
The Africans bellow...

We stop our
tale at that
and reckon with the white
narrative bleep
impenetrable as fog
paper pregnant with script.

I've an uncle, said he'd
eat nothing that come out the sea.
Couldn't stomach black bone broth
coursing through fish gills,
sand, sediment, onyx, and bone.

Belly up starfish seaweed tangle
barged wood barnacle visage.

The count impossible to make
said I was a made man when
she launched her schooner
from the business end
of a four poster bed.

The New World is the way
of the waving arm that morphs to fist
conch shell viciously blown
The dance of machetes

Faces swolled up
by brine
           by bile

Bludgeoned memory,

a song carried
caressed

in a sling stone loaded.

Black canaries
feathering the dark

Dis/tune of mind/e
this/dis place that breaks
the black/nest of sparks

|

Daddy   was   a
Burner   of   Bridges

Circa nineteen and seventy grilled

                                                at the corner of Fifth & Jefferson
window or repo
you don't know

watch repair shop & hey slick
you my main man   so cut me some slack

and give me the brothers' discount
on this here Timex cause
                                                I could
                                                use a brew with the extra change

(He plan on laying down five
                on Black Betty.)

                Daddy was a talker straight out the gate

Overdue by late night blow
by blare of rickety
RCAs that piped in Hi Karate,
Pal Malls, red car dreams & late night sign offs
with Blue Angel music

(He was a lucky son of a bitch and when Betty hit we was all gentrification and gratitude.)

Looked like a raincloud of quarters
A hail storm of dimes
A drizzle of nickels

                                        Once under the vertical and horizontal comets

flashing their way across glass
He leaned over in his arm chair
said to me "Damn Major Ant
hony for passin' up Jeannie
's good pus
sy."

How to be Remembered

a name—a date—a place—a year—a day—a month—a century—an epoch—a season—a surname—
a middle initial—a first name—an occupation—a quote—a place to drop flowers—
a ridge of stone—a seed of bone—a mound—a knee bent to ground—a section—a locale—
a pastoral ridge—a road to drive to—a plot—a thickening—a tear—a tear—a lawn manicured—
a special tree—a special plea—a seclusion—a sedation—a seduction—a will—a testament—
a bridge—a finality—a cough—a recognizable sniffle—a special suit—a subdued tie—
a receding hair line—a brown shoe—a brown shoe—a black belt—a wedding ring—
a carnation—a pair of glasses—a handkerchief—a stiff upper lip—a stiff upper lip—
a flask—a memorial program—a church fan—a hearse's engine—a white cloud overhead—
a fallen leaf—a sudden bird song—a sun in the branches—a nugget of dirt—a sprinkler—
a lawn mower—a funeral flag—a random bicyclist—a black gate—a black gait—a record—
a capacity—a requiem—a window—a windbag—a slight—a slip—a read—a reed—
a rhapsody—a lapel—a brush—a flaw—a spare—a sparkle—a spandex—a crown—a castanet—
a eulogy—a feud—a flood—a stamp—a cellular text—a sandwich—a candy bar—
a bag of nuts—a casserole—a potted plant—a creeping moss—a caterpillar—a cocoon—
a loose thread—a sweaty armpit—a cigarette stub—a loose quarter—a bottle of pills—
a veil—a hat band—a line of reasoning—a contract—a contact—a religious medal—
a lawyer—a widow—a survivor—a shovel—a pulley—a glove—a dog—a beetle—
a business card—a repass—a nickel—a sneeze—a cough—a lien—a reunion—
a genealogy—a claimant—a brick pathway—a curb—an abode—a body—a body—a body—

The   Opening   Salvo

Blood reign
snow/rain

oh the meteoritic conditions outside are frightful
and the combustion is so delightful

"So what" says Miles Davis.

and I couldn't really give a shit about that seersucker wearing muthafucka

                                  The stereo is bleeding

and the needle is slanted
where Devonte is poised to hear
                his heart's jazz.

                                  Poised to where?
                                  I rarely see anyone
                                  outside of myself
                                  without the accompanying
                                  etiquette of propriety.

Momentary lapse, a complaint

                ((Miniscule really, something that doesn't escape the aficionado's ear
             (the perfect   example of Modal jazz in the Dorian mode))
                        a compliance
                                in the music
comply with me

Cannonball picks up the attack
The needle glides, the speakers rumble
a vein tapped to rise
burnt point juncture bruise
beaten up behind the beat down and out *beat me daddy eight to the bar*

Come on, come on try to keep up with this shit

A note locks in
sound is immaculate
at times inarticulate.

                                  Night lapses into nonsense
                                  can be noose if we lack
                                  the necessary vigilance

(frontal cortex, nucleus accumbens, ventral tegmental
area) dopamine tide, javelin
junkie nod.

By now the needle bobs back and forth
sound is crackle, electro fuzz

There's a horn outside
but not the kind you'd expect.

It's a car calling
a tenant to work. She's getting in
now, dragging on the stub of her
cigarette.

Devonte drifts in and out of sleep.
He speaks a cartography of allusions:

I moan the mourning
(scratch the face)
the moor to man
(scratch the face)
the Desdemona fix where whatever
cues my aspiration
(scratch the face)

What I need here is image
wide-ranged & split-open
a calculation of weights
to pounce a solid punch.
                    —*Net of Empire: The Writer's Dream*

The   Alley   Prowler

Where he weighs

                                         what to do
                                         how to set it straight
                                         find a place sweet
                                         spot foretold a weight
                                         to strike it rich
                                         like a phantom hand
                                         stroking a five-percenter's goatee

"Whatever"
           says the blade
"Whoever"
           says the jersey shoe (shore)

Hasty recall repaved
                   a scene 'cross his shaven pate
he said so she said little

Not that difference could hold
them apart
from the other sharp
articulation of the scalpel's art

                                         delinquent date of which
                                         he wasn't quite sure.

The fix was in   the saucy puddle
wrench coat   and brine disguise

Who sat engrossed by the old mill stream?
Was it a carbuncle of tin pan alley songsters?

                             Surely her and not mother engorged
                             by her constant complaints

Still the dream of her
under a myriad of lights
to mean knights here.

Devonte's the kind of brother
who'd give you the spirit
off his back if you would ask

Fashion a divining rod from epileptic antennas
Pilgrimage the urban nerve in
search of the opiate vein
meaning the music,
                         hear?

"Farmed out to who?
Come on Isabelle,
you playin' me for a mantis?
a gardenia bulb bludgeoned shut?
a tsunami throbbing under an eyelid?"

Devonte scuffles in the alley
with a shadow, trips tying his shoe.

Out here, he's a crack Casanova,
a bloated gosling bobbing in the silt.

He regards the flame in his hand

primes his throat,

walks the accusatory road.

Devonte   Wakes
from   a   Dream

Gauze of night:

I am the luminary
cuddled in vortex spin
of my left eye

ripe with sheep corpses.

I am the solitary

conch of weeping
dominos and crucifixes
of burning bibles.
Bed linen of tongues
quilt of bones,

I hewn and mine from   Nut's celestial pillow

the uterus of sleep
a scimitar of fables
a booty of furry beasts
and a scaffold of bodies to mount
launch my intent from the isthmus of faucets
in basalt speckled word-sand.

My legacy is a knapsack
of whispering cowrie shells

My lineage sprawls the shore
of an indigo sea

where I will
dance with
Erzulie,
take in
the beauty of her eyes
be blessed
by the aqua-blue trinity
of her shimmering rings.

What the Medicine Cabinet Said

Devonte, think of it this way
    that the   faces   of gods

              are hidden   in the bathroom orchids.

Believe you me   I've seen them

                        silently whispering through the shampoo smoke
    the aftershave offerings

                          that waft over our lady of the toilet

above the hydrogenous fissures   we mistake for mouths
above   the hand   that trembles

before unscrewing   the aspirin host
                    above the mouthwash

with its undeniable

periwinkle for cleanliness
the commode gods are staring.

              They are contemplating
              your next awkward preamble.

They are waiting
to pounce forth from
the moan and sway
of your bowels,
eating away at you like
maggots devouring flesh.

Devonte   Travels
the   Sorry   Route

True, like I scribe to you
Devonte was a foot soldier.
Hep to the old one two
brogan banged pavement.

Downbeat long past
"feets do yo stuff."
He was the dis
mordant shuffler,
son of the penny-ante,
off-beat "love will find a way" Blakean prodigy.

                                        Gilder of man
                                        holes and jack-ball
                                        bottles pushed to the curb.

He was the hoofer,
the wolf boy calling cadence
to Okmulgee back
dreams and dawning days
where he Eagle Rocked
in Cimarron sludge
and ragged tails   at a high school dance

After hours
            Devonte pushed a rickety shopping cart
                                through market lanes and stone soul picnic
surrey with the frontier fringe on top.
emblematic of the colonizer's booze
grandiloquent booby prize filth
                        progeny of branch noose ripe tree

Legacy of a miraculous
bounty of hang nailed fingers
blood birds poaching pedigrees to
"Here I am. Now you see me, now you don't."
subject to the gaze of distant blue hated brothers
or rather a bother of continual apparition

the "me not me" rattling in the stove pipe
of his own voice rife with suffering.

A Miraculous Coat of Arms

                                          Black, blue, discombobulated, and disembodied
                                          a phantom limb slinks behind Devonte's back.

One would think then, his body
has slipped, was splayed out by sleight of hand,

the expectant rabbit secreted under top hat
chomping at the bit
of earth root, gold carrot & bountiful crotch
jokingly called fruit of the loon
bent this feathered horn to the wind

                                                        To hear what?

Saint and sinners praising?

But the ownerless hand gestures the balm of "I love you"

As if the torture of protracted angles
and gushing fissures of color
were not enough to supply the narrative with forethought

                                                  But the nob points downward

as if to say I love this earth

Desire to roil in its majestic sieve
top soil worms, acorns with jagged fissures,
decaying bird or grub, mole flung

                              Who brings the trough
                              to cradle and silence the earth's womb?

This be our species greed, this adaptability to malady.
Volition of the evolutionary law Darwin holds aloft.

                                        What is survival's fittest?

Is it the ancestral side-step when point of origin blinks?

Is it the waistcoat one fashions at the toilet mirror?

Or the side-long glance of upturned heel on pavement word?

                              & what of this Devonte, bubonic albino
                              traversing between the parameters of race?

Yes, once the skin is flayed . . .

The phantom limb
always extends downward.
Pointer to our need
for closure.

This dictation
giving way
to direction.

A   Fine   Education,
Mr.   Devonte

"An American is a complex of occasions."
Charles Olson

What does it mean to be a stalker of history?

Devonte was faced with that question.
All through school the truth was elusive.

Placed between the covers of state sponsored books,
they contained a series of dates and numbers, hints of atrocities,

records of plagues, sutures, speculums,
cranial calipers, petri dish DNA, fetuses in jars,

exfoliated skulls, hands sprouting with dark veins
blunt presurgical tools, towers of limbs, jaundiced femurs,

rib cages wracked by disease,
nooses, rusted shackles, indigenous meat,

gasoline martyrs, electric chair voltage,
hydrochloric cleansing, chambers of vapor,

police batons and hoses, lye and quicklime,
rabid coonhounds, bullwhips,

cat-o'-nine-tails, stacks of penises, chopped breasts,
sun swollen tongues, animal fur and talons,

identity cards of gonorrhea,
leather-bound family bibles,

carbines and swords, smallpox laden blankets,
maps and portraits, places of conquest,

outcroppings, shattered rocks,
felled timber, inventory of a nation,

a place to lay identity at the foot of *I am this,*
that, the other and all things are contained therein.

*

I wanted to remain anonymous
                not seen, the animal inside
                                the pageant of fangs poised to blood

wanted to be anecdotal roaring
                tail by fire told to menacing embers
                                told to steel poker with chattel prod

wanted to be avatar
                wanted to be cinnamon and brown
                                night not this one not this one

wanted to be the hail from the grove
                the albatross refusing to land
                                wanted to be karaoke and polestar

compass and cypress wanted to be fire chain
                or burnt sienna brush obliterating canvas
                                wanted to be carve and carry

stones of gull wall
                wanted hand to masque
                                hatchling of maggots in crow's nest

wanted to sprout my sundial decay
                as far as my foot's cerebellum.

Devonte   Recalls
the   Hard   Lesson

Calley's dancin' in My Lai
Calley's dancin' in My Lai
Lord, Lord got to get my boots 'way from here
                —Trad.

Like a figure outward (bowsprit?)
the limbs first present themselves as sea seasoned meat

Contrast to the starch white of navy issue breeches
and good ship lollypop chapeaus

Devonte's one good leg sports shackle or shale cuff
on the phantom other, the unmentionable flint of tribal imagination
                Perhaps a watering can flowering neither funeral rite nor flower

Great and celebrated admiral of the sea
weed and rank latrine your boots are stolid
markers and the shoreline marks the trajectory
of dark holds
and blood razed riggings

Your waistcoat is a dung beetle carapace

                Your brass buttons are a lineage of skull tureens

They are your family totem,
the blue-eyed fledglings you've abandoned to home.

"I'm impaled by the word's molten poker.
My skin peels to coffee-au-lait.
                I'm your prize parakeet
                your sage singing sambo."

It was here Devonte realized that his
altercation is with history circa 1968
not the sweet cinderblocks laid to his head
by a congenial crew of petty teachers
and pate fed administrators.

                And oh the songs we raised from our juvenile chests
                under the banner of gym light and bleacher.
                for god, for country, words we forgot
                this pigment of rote while the hamlets burned.

Devonte's   Dyscalculia
(1 + 6 + 3 + 2 = 1 2)

Not good at calculus,
god, nor metaphysical restraint

Devonte momentarily reclined
on a divan, imagining himself
a giant hen with a calendar full of

egg brimming peepers.

The apostolic twelve hung precariously in the canvas
overhead as he lackadaisically lapsed into
a baptismal dreary while pondering
a Christ fugue he had constructed in his head.

But he was too far from the Steinway
to spew the artfully poised tune.

"No Count" was something his father had called
him, "No Count
on account of you're wasting time.
Seven days a week baby,
a paper boy on a bicycle.

That white canvas bag the envy of the route less
They'd all look sleepy eyed out of their windows.

I would be morning rise wheel cacophony.
Handlebar totter burned ked rubber with none the wiser."

What boots we all have to live up to
thought Devonte, *dainty and white at first*
then supple leather, then car boot, funeral boot
and all life diminished in one rosy prison dream

"Sure," he muses "6" *to mean six feet under.*

The preacher's last handful of dirt and ash.

Not Pythagoras's perfect digit or I-Ching heaven

I am the "1" ekah, universality, spirit, the divine.
The Axis Mundi whether I lie vertical or horizontal,

Then "3" be trinity, jeweled refuge of Buddha, Dharma, Sangha
the cosmic pulse of Bird, Trane and Ayler
                                    explosive in the eye of a cat caught in moonlit glare.

Devonte repositions his body on the divan,
musters off his weight and makes a move toward the piano
plunks down two fingers to make a blurred middle C.

Then "2" is the positive and negative of all aspects.

It is me and my father at the mirror
the two faces I can't shake.

Not Abbot and Costello's first
nor Gertrude's knock-kneed Napoleonic twist
but the covert rhythm of Devonte's heart
cascaded, no arabesqued really
at the suggestion of her name.

> Twas no gibbous moon, nor Moorish noontide
> when he conjured her, rhapsodic under
> the stately elm at Bearden Park.

Tubers of prophylactics littered the grass.
Cacti of thirsty syringes accused the sky,
mangled his dreams when she came crashing into him.
He lifted his hand to his jaw. Did the junkie scratch,
gingerly darted his tongue back
and forth across his lips.

A procession of ants masquerading as a shoe lace.
A dime a dozen. A shift in scene to well-quaffed
colonial hybrids answering nature's call to fetch.

> *In the painting "1632"*
> *appears. Can we assume*
> *the artist (Counihan?) has*
> *indicated a particular hist-*
> *orical eddy? Did he employ*
> *his brushes to traverse time?*

"See the number that hovers in the corner?"

> *What number?*

"There. See it?"

> *...an entity hovers beneath the sheets...*

> *What coroner? What depth?*

> *Where to lay my axes*
> *or the box with my father's ashes.*
> *There is no churning sea*
> *and all my countrymen are apparitions*
> *and my house / homeland burns.*

"Milquetoast" Isabelle ascribes to Devonte.

She, the color of dead,
nails long enough
to reel him in.

Devonte's   Toast

"De system is a fraud."
—Mutabaruka

Dis man's speech

(The dining table was the lectern. Oil portraits of founders hung in funeral splendor.
Devonte marveled how their lineage of greed was captured between gilded frames and
fleur-de-lis wallpaper. Then he noticed the ornate bowls brimming with cane and blood.)

What they want is a smiling darkie
                        one who wipes the sweat
off his handkerchief
                        holds up the golden horn
with an Uncle Ben smile
                        and a band of bucks

[Keeper of syncopation]

But that ain't what they got behind the
grin and the gin done got me mad
sayin' fuck you and your music
I'm here to tell you
to kiss my black bottom

                                    [certainly the hostess was greatly offended]

& when Dis man was done
firing up the bowl
of invectives
they were the ones
doin' the scraping, the bowing, the smiling

"After all we've done for him."

            "He should be grateful."

                        "I even had him over for dinner."

Nick knack paddy whack!
Now who's got
the fuckin' bone?

Devonte was in a parlor (a paradox)
a paramour a pompadour
a pair of doc martens candy stripe shoelaces
scalpels ready
then she waltzed in whistling
pomp and circumstance

          substantiated by the sequin gown she wore.
"Reclining" is the word
her colonial daddies would have slathered.

        But were it for the strain of her mammary (no, memory) …
        No, the stain of her curses slapped against his cheek …

        [A billiards table
        held the dead man.]

"Tell me again doll face that I'm the winning hazard
carom to your father's bald head."
Devonte's inclined

              to rack him up,
              hoist a shot of Dickel
              & drown in the
              geometry of her eyes.

"Regale me with how
your story ends sweetheart
& leaves you stateless."

              How could he have known
               that he was her candidate,
                  her golden boy

       under the cursive curve of neon lights
         stiletto heels, gleaming smile?

"Baby, I'm the sucker, the solitary chrysanthemum,
the big bar stogie stank."

         Why is it they can't face each other
         with the gaze of conspiratorial murderer
         amongst legions of button

         down coats, scarlet blouses, and banked
         shots?

                              Was it something Isabelle did not say when
                              she held his trembling hand against the
                              candle's flame and told
                              him, her blue is the color of rain?

There is a dead man here (her father)
and all the angels tonight
are racking balls,
chalking cues and coughing blood.

Their pronouncements pressed
the holy wafers of fortune on our tongues
the car-lit pavement outside spattered
                              with tomorrow's headlines.

Strange   Fruit

For Isabelle, Tugger of Brushes

Reflect on this   then   my beloved:

a *Golden Delicious apple*
(artfully hung)
precariously poised
        on bee blossom bearing limbs   ^above us^

Consider velocity   pro-jec-tile   per-cus-sive
potent weight
        wait, no wait   no, wattage   no, wind gate
no breed mare as words
                            worlds? this fruit proposes

Uncomplicated, Newtonian red cape,
white scalloped pantaloons
shoe buckles glossy with gravitas spit (gravity,   no gravy,   no gringo
no grocer, no glockenspiel
) Leibniz's London mud

                    [You tell me you've had enough of this pondering
                    & we let fall the apple, constellations drape night sky.]

Darling, we two are snared
in this immense cosmic fabric
myopic corneas caught
                in each glaucomic glance
                in each cataract of untamed lids
                in each cartouche of optic nerves

It's a fruit fly's wing gauze,
the transparent breath
of its midair turbulence
that erupts the foreboding spring.

                        It's a dervish spinning counter clockwise
                        in the hint of a sand storm.
                        It's the smoky infusion of quartz and mica
                        that guards the entrance to the caves
                        of oblivion.

It's wave foam the frothy locks of Agwé
threatening to swallow us whole
It's a cornucopia of moons set before us
in a basket woven by emerald hummingbirds.

It's my grandmother handing me
the knife of my ancestry

                       and telling me that the apple's golden skin
                       contains the fruit of my fathomless salvation.

Devonte Sports a Canvas

Rendered, not wrought, he
strikes the Toussaint pose.

    Serpentine in tri-cornered hat
    reluctant general more rather

        Banger of midnight bedpans
        & leaden walks to the latrine.

            Perhaps it was the vinegaresque
            vintage distilled from Haitian cane.

                He has a house on his head, a domicile
                for mother rocking in curds & weighted bluster.

                    He swallows the Bastille & swirls his tongue
                    as if it were a stitch of cholera

                        Caught in guillotine blade.
                        His nose is a blunderbuss,

                            his ear a Tin Pan Alley nail.

                            Devonte shadows his familiar
                            a worn man shackled to a pleading look.

[Counihan slathers pigment.]

[He wants nothing to do with this art.]

In   the   Crow's   Nest

Atmospheric   almost   rapier.
Proposition to aspire to.
Perhaps gecko tutelary tongue
precarious rigging climb

Measurer of footholds lest he plummet
where horizon meets hydrogenous eye.
Attempts to be leveler

                                                            [imagine would be leviathan]
                                                            ]

Devonte straddles the breezeway,
whistler of diasporic shanties recently cuffed
from history books to his ankle like
"no" he couldn't imagine the glissando
finger sprits of Isabelle, Tugger of Brushes.

                                        Hair as black as a port,
                                        as a port,
                                        as a Port u guese,
                                        as a Portuguese
                                        man-of-war or her
                                        mercurial polishing
                                        of pearly whites

                                                    the very same skulls
                                        he dreams littering the Atlantic.

Before night table light extinguished
Before the phantom luminosity
of an alarm sets the measure
her brownstone murky depth
fifth floor where she plots her playthings scattered
Oh Columbia, Gem of the Ocean
harbinger of serpents blood jeweled.

*

In barnacle pocked ports, in warehouses, in barns they were herded like oxen.
Forced to present their orifices to the puerile whim of spectacle and glove
where the warp and weave of cloth snags the good word.

*

How does one enter a doorway,
hoist a spyglass to a jaundiced eye?

How does one siege and pillage a body
festering with eclipsed moons?

Momma, how does one set sail clipper to sea, voyage unknown
an abyss of uncharted stars hung up to hamper your way?

The Sari Root Unravels

Blue, I'm a scribe to you,
a sari wearing foot soldier.
Amenhotep the old one-two
bargain the beguine
down streets long past "frets do thy stuff."

I'm the diatonic shifter,
sun son of the anti-panty,
the off-beat Reichian prodigy.
Guilder of mammoths
and jack-balled babies pushing erb,

I'm the woofer, the wool-
eyed boy whistling "Candide."
to oatmeal black dreams and drawing days
where I Eagle Rocked in cinnamon sludge
and ragged trails at a high school dance.

After hours I push a rickety shopping cart
through Kasbah lanes and stone sold pillars
sari with the fringe on top.

Emblem of the coroner's blues,
a dilettante's booty prize filched,
my progeny of blanched nuts and raped trees
my legacy of Miranda's rites
and a bevy of hang-nailed fugues.

Blood poachers to pedophiles to "Here I am.
Now you see me, now you don't."

Subject to the gaze of distance
or rather the continental appropriations
of the "me not me" bubbling up in the spine crack of
my back, bent with singing.

Devonte
the

Exhumes
Archive

With the library window open
an angry rain came blowing in.

D thought about the ancestors
the kind and straight ones

stately in their white wraps
their flowing garments

of course there were

children as well

unknowing & innocent

I set my course
atop the curve of Atlantic wave
cleave to the thought
of return to palm frond shores
of hermit crabs burrowing
in Afric sand.

My people, my people
lost to text and ink
(the book's tyranny)

[The light is bad.
His eyes conspire to
subvert his attempt
to decipher the yellowing
parchment.]

Dear Isabelle,
    If you are reading this letter now
then you will know I have
already departed for the abyss.
As I have neither map nor compass,
do not expect to find me
or hear from me for that matter.
My fortune lies with space
the open cosmic frame.
I suckle on the teats of Nut.
"I am one with the sound eye.
Even when closed I'm in its protection."

(De vo nte coul dno t m ak eout thes ignat ure.
He coul dno t re cog nize the cur sive curl
of hiso w n h and.)

                             ...and a tight fitting bodice
                             by fire by stain by beer

                *

Do you see the bloated bodies Devonte?
the serenades of weight and balance?
the ballast that haunts this soul ship?

For me my tale developed
in a glade of driftwood above sea spray assault
by the cliffs of her penciled eyebrows
by the massive sails of her chest
by the coughing of blood and barnacle
by the compass that sprouts needles
into the forearms of a sitar.

The pane of the library window is cracking.
It is turning into a jagged smile.

Wake up Devonte. Wake up!

The Alchemical   Chimera's Vibe

If you are sitting on the porch
                If you are on a swing,
                                If you are on a porch swing

If you are in the sun in sunlight
                                                on a green porch swing
                                                somewhere in the south
Southern exposure and sitting

on a green porch swing.

Taking a poached swig a brew that bakes
the dermal edges of the head
articulates where the music is to go
rhythmic drive where the drummer
stirs up trouble with his divining sticks.

                                The atmosphere was auspicious
                                A moment when no thing
                                could hamper the potent mixture of sound.

To a degree Devonte was calling up
unfamiliar agents, specters of people
long gone, barefoot and road walking among the clouds

Some of them carried root loaded knapsacks
drawings and daguerreotypes of loved ones lost.
What was the mixture that he saw?
Brew of brood, body doubled?

                                The elements conspired against
                                a narrative consistency of need

It was tasteful to a degree, mirthful even
that moment when smoke shapes
itself into animal and object.

                                A way to read the projective (perspective)
                                before things, the nature of which
                                resolves to dust.

On the eaves of the porch
a glimmering chimera sat in judgement.
Sulfuric snot drifted out from her nostril.

Devonte witnessed the gravity
of the situation and satisfied himself
to be adrift in the lostness of primal cauldrons.

The The of Sacred Anansian Initiate Society Scribes

We do not really mean, we do not really mean that what we are about to say is true. A story, a story; let it come, let it go.

Note: The Sacred Society of Anansian Scribes initiation opens with the blowing of the conch shell, followed by a succession of call-and-response from drummers. The ceremony can occur only on the new moon of the vernal equinox. It must be performed near a body of water. Prior to the initiation the oldest member of the Society writes the symbolic names of the initiate's ancestral line in a circle of sand. As each initiate arrives, they crawl counter clockwise over the symbols until they are no longer recognizable (the symbols and the initiate). All eight Anansian priests must be present for the ceremony to be valid.

Aunt Nancy:
(Lights torch and raises arms)
We are limbs from Anansi's
spider underground.

Priests:
(Bow to Aunt Nancy)
We sing a diasporic shanty
amidst the layers of Western dung.

Initiate:
(Bows to altar, bows to priests)
I anoint myself with porpoise oil
and await instructions from the tide.
Mother Anansi who impregnates the solar ovum.

Priests:
(Dance with grotesque gestures)
We buck dance the cakewalk
on our backs ridged with the railroads
of volcanoes.

Initiate:
(Picks up a machete and imitates priests' dance and bows)
I am of the underground union cypher and spinsters
weavers at the barricades
stitchers of cowrie threaded heads.

Priests:
(Bow to initiate)
Our teeth tear at the flesh of language
disembowel the syntax writhing
in the shackles of your impotent catechisms.
We launch a logos of froth
the script of blood's holy feast

Initiate:
(Returns bow)
I, the underground mandible
of mollusks and mosques,
the gut stringed throat that launches
a thousand spasms articulating
the insurrection of malarial flowers.

Aunt Nancy:
(Bows twice to the four directions, shake calabash rattle 8xs)
This cataclysm marks
your auspicious arrival.

This is my story which I have related. If it be sweet, or if it be not sweet, take some elsewhere, and let some come back to me.

Legba was there,
as was *Thoth*,
Anansi, and *Ani*,
the scribe.

[There were others whose names
stem from the tongues of vanished people.]

*We come from a long line of observers,
recorders of act and intention.*

*The scrolls are the coils of Damballa,
umbilical, continual ingestion.*

*We play to the heart beat of all things
that dictate the parameters of dance.*

Devonte had lost control of his legs.

His knees would dip in sporadic fits.
His arms would wildly whirl above his head
& he could feel the stretch
of muscle and cartilage.

Possessed, he was mounted by
what seemed to be letters.
Some he could identify,
others he could not.

Veins in his neck pulsed.
Sound bubbled from the ground
made its way to his mouth.
Pushed his breath out
then exited
like lava.

He took on different poses:
Adopted the gestures of African
gods in the dark holds
of New World bound ships.

The vigor of writing
is not in how one wields the pen
but how one captures
the merger of mind and language.

Devonte prepares his writing armaments
for the battle knowing he will lose.
What is writing but a struggle to employ
the limits of speech?

What whirls around you is
best captured by a guttural grunt.
So what.

Ancestors   Are   Calling

Sometimes the ancestors call

                              tongue to mouth
                              an auburn molt of daguerreotypes stained

Sometimes the ancestors call

                              an earwig gracefully arranged
                              a pebble between pincers caught
                              is the scene's composition

Sometimes the ancestors call

                              shovel heeled curt wedge of earth,
                              a convent of daises assaulted
                              a lunar moth poised at dung end
                              oak leaf suddenly caught at mid-fall

Sometimes the ancestors call
                              dark sip sickle scythe curve
                              a wagon's tracks from coffins weighed

Wind to forecast their arrival
Wind to dictate the shuffle
and strut of steps
to the rust of gates.

Sometimes the ancestors call

Not in the great cinematographic arias
of gun firing bandits at a locomotive's gray smoke
but in rage of gray starlings
circling over head

Not in the paranoia of walks down bug house corridors
Nor to bed pans brimmed do they call.
Not in the paranormal cadences
                    of cathedral spiked with sepulcher and crucifix

I could be anything
other than what I propose here

                        I could be song

                                  I could be dance

                                            I could be slab of sky

How many generations still left to measure?
At what cost this cadence?
At what price the grave's granite thumb?

Murky with Delinquent Notes
We Insist! Freedom Now Suite

But, I am looking
                    not at you   but rather
through you
                                    with your butter brimming Aunt Jemimas
in the dew-rag dawn
of maple syrup
                slave shack to
log cabin to
shake master's breakfast in a quake
                        in a Quaker Oats shuffle
a soufflé of indigo screams.

The whip of cane by sugar harvested.   This machete to cut my way through
                        the dense verbiage of your language.

With your molars grinding   the morning assault
of yet another
newspaper splattered with black   body counts.

        I got a shitload of loose coffee pebbles
that need to be reconciled.

        I got Uncle Ben's rice converted
to a Congo harvest ripe with severed hands.

                                    I wield an incendiary device birthed from
                                    glossaries of impending legislation afloat in
                                    my speech.

                                    I am a Blue Mountain Maroon torching your
                                    stereos
                                    roasting your genital tongues.

I am just around the corner where
boys play hoop
& leave the ball midair

                        They are the basket weavers,
                        the showboaters,
                        tail spin and wolf
                        fake to the right

then the twirl behind
the back jazz body aesthetic
smoke and mirrors
Anansi's arrival.

That's the court
I pledge allegiance to.

I am looking   beyond
the blind gloss of fruited plains
                         the huddled masses yearning
for holiday cakes

                                    and fuel efficient ballads.

Take note, I sport a bandoleer
of guttural scat
staccatos of soaked Max sticks.
Baby, I'm a mean bone slinger
with an Abbey wail
and my cleanup will be messy.

i

where do I
divine myself
here in the clothes
of words

ii

sometimes
anything can be
a vessel the rough
beach bone sand
sculpted knot
drifting word

iii

words are particles
hard carved scroll
on cherry banister
valise expectant
of yellowed papers
or perhaps a solitary castanet,
a cumulus of foam formed
over the Atlantic shoulder or
your glasses of fashion decayed

iv

the look so perfect
after the suspect "oh"
this dream
an alchemic equation.

Dedication

I am the grateful recipient of tremendous support from family and friends. The names of my many benefactors are too numerous to place here. I don't want to omit anybody. Recognizing the limits of space, and I mean that in more ways than one, I want all of you to know that I am appreciative of those shared meals, sublime concerts, energetic classrooms, spontaneous conversations, city walks, country hikes, long drives, and ancestral calling drum circles. Please know that I know who you are and that I am well aware that your engagement and encouragement were the catalysts for what you hold in your hands. Thank you!

Again, my boundless gratitude goes out to Pauline Kaldas, and my daughters Yasmine and Celine.